Jesus: The Hope of Easter

The Story of the Resurrection

Authored and Illustrated by

Lenora Murdock

© 2024

All rights reserved.

Murdock

Dedicated to Julia and Millie.
My heart and inspiration to share
hope the hope of Scripture.

Over 2000 years ago, in a land filled with sunshine and olive groves, lived a special man named Jesus. He wasn't a king or a knight, but he did amazing things! Jesus was the very son of God, sent from Heaven.

He was kind and wise. He healed the sick, comforted the sad, and taught people about love, kindness, and forgiveness.

Everyone called him "Teacher," and his words filled their hearts with hope.

One day, Jesus visited Jerusalem, a bustling city filled with people from all corners of the land. As he neared the city gates, something incredible happened!

Jesus rode into Jerusalem, riding humbly on a donkey, smiling warmly at everyone. He felt their love and knew they saw the hope he carried.

Children ran excitedly, tossing flowers at his feet, while adults spread their cloaks on the ground for him to walk on.
It was like a giant, happy parade, welcoming their beloved Teacher.

The people thought Jesus would save them from their harsh rulers, but Jesus's mission was even greater than that!

Not everyone shared their joy. Some powerful people felt threatened by his teachings and secretly planned to stop him.

One night Jesus gathered his twelve closest friends for a special meal. They broke bread and shared wine, celebrating love and their friendship with Jesus.

It was a night filled with some of Jesus' most important teachings. With a gentle sadness, Jesus shared that he wouldn't be with them much longer.

The night deepened, and fear crept in. But Jesus reassured them, his voice steady and kind. "Remember my teachings, my friends," he said. "Have faith, even when things seem scary. Together, we'll see the light shine again."

These words, filled with love and hope, became a beacon in the darkness, guiding them through the coming storm.

Later that night, in a quiet garden filled with olive trees, Jesus went to pray. But he wasn't alone. The friend who planned to betray him, Judas, led a group of soldiers to the garden.

Their torches flickered through the trees. With a kiss in the darkness, Judas revealed who Jesus was. The soldiers grabbed him. They took him away, even though he hadn't done anything wrong.

But even as they were scattered, Jesus's teachings of love, forgiveness, and hope echoed in his disciple's hearts. These words would guide them through the darkest nights.

Imagine a tall wooden cross, like a big X. Some people wanted to punish Jesus and put him on the cross, even though he hadn't hurt anyone. It was a very scary and sad time for Jesus and his friends, but Jesus never stopped being kind. He even forgave those who hurt him.

As the sun dipped low, the sky turned dark and gloomy. The ground shook, and even the sun seemed to hide. Jesus, hanging on the cross, spoke his last words of love and forgiveness before closing his eyes. It felt like everything good had ended.

His friends and followers felt lost without their dear Teacher. But three days later something miraculous happened! Early in the morning, the ground rumbled and a giant rock blocking a cave where Jesus was laid to rest suddenly rolled away.

His friends couldn't believe it at first. But then, guess who they saw walking towards them? Jesus! He was alive, healthy, and smiling! He had conquered death and returned, just like he promised.

News of Jesus's return spread like wildfire. People who had heard his teachings but doubted him now knew it was true. Jesus was the Son of God. His love and kindness triumph over everything, even death!

His friends, filled with joy, shared the story with everyone. This story reminds us that there's always light and hope waiting around the corner. It's a reminder to be kind, forgiving, and loving like Jesus, who showed us the greatest love of all. It's a story that fills our hearts with hope!

So, whenever you feel sad or scared, remember Jesus's story. Remember that love and hope always win, just like the bright sunshine after a rainy day!

And because of his special love, Jesus did something amazing! He promised that after life here on Earth ends, his friends could join him in a beautiful place called Heaven, filled with joy and peace. It's like a giant, happy adventure that never ends!

All you have to do is believe in him. He called this special promise "eternal life," because it meant being together forever, even after our earthly journey is complete.

Though many years have passed, Jesus promise still holds true. He wants everyone to share in this incredible gift, including you!

So remember, whenever you feel lost or scared, hold onto his love and believe in his promise. Trust in his kindness, and follow his teachings of love and forgiveness. Jesus offers hope that can guide you through any darkness, towards a future filled with love, peace, and joy, forever and always.

Jesus said, "I am the resurrection and the life. Anyone who believes in me will live, even when this earthly journey is over. Everyone who believes in me will never ever die.

John 11:25-26

Because I live, you also will live.

John 14:19

Made in the USA
Las Vegas, NV
16 March 2024